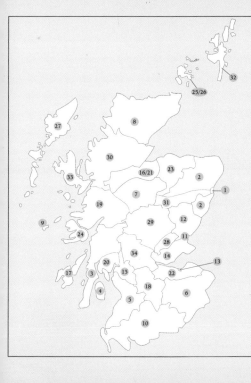

1. Aberdeen
2. Aberdeenshi...
3. Argyll
4. The Isle of ...
5. Arran & A...
6. The Bord...
7. The Cair...
8. Caithness & Sutherland
9. Coll & Tiree
10. Dumfries & Galloway
11. Dundee
12. Dundee & Angus
13. Edinburgh
14. Fife, Kinross & Clackmannan
15. Glasgow
16. Inverness
17. Islay, Jura, Colonsay & Oronsay

26. Orkney ...
27. The Outer Hebrides
28. The City of Perth
29. Highland Perthshire
30. Ross & Cromarty
31. Royal Deeside
32. Shetland
33. The Isle of Skye
34. Stirling & The Trossachs

The remaining six books, *Caledonia*, *Distinguished Distilleries*, *Sacred Scotland*, *Scotland's Mountains*, *Scotland's Wildlife* and *The West Highland Way* feature locations in various parts of the country, so are not included in the map list above.

PICTURING SCOTLAND

MORAY-SPEYSIDE

COLIN NUTT
Author and photographer

2   A panoramic view of Lossiemouth beach and the River Lossie estuary.

MORAY-SPEYSIDE

Welcome to Moray!

The modern-day county of Moray encompasses as wide a variety of scenery and depth of history as any part of Scotland. The boundary changes of 1974 saw it absorb the southern part of neighbouring Banffshire and this greatly expanded the 'new' county's geographical range. However, in recent times the branding of *Historic Banffshire* has been created and applied to the relevant areas, highlighted by roadside signs.

Thanks to the 1974 re-organisation, the south-western boundary of Moray passes through the Cairngorms summits of Cairn Gorm and Ben Macdui (second highest mountain in Britain). From this 1220m/4000ft plateau, Moray sweeps down Strath Avon and Glen Livet to glorious Speyside, world-renowned for its salmon fishing and malt whisky. Speyside has the greatest concentration of malt whisky producers compared to every other whisky-producing region. Moray also lost some territory to the same boundary changes, its former south-western corner being taken into Highland Region. This included the town of Grantown-on-Spey, so in acknowledgement of its recent past and to allow inclusion of more of Speyside, this book will stretch a point and visit that area too.

As the county unfolds from the mountains to the sea, it embraces rich farmland that produces an abundance of crops, including the top-quality barley needed by the distilleries. The richness of the land has meant that Moray has been home to humankind for at least four millennia.

Moray begins here! The county's western boundary runs through the summits of Cairn Gorm and Ben Macdui, forming an arc around lovely Loch Avon, seen here.

The Picts ('painted people') have left dramatic evidence of their occupancy of the region: one of the most magnificent Pictish standing stones in Europe has been re-erected in Forres. Standing over 6m/20ft tall, Sueno's Stone was unearthed in 1726 and is estimated to have been carved in the 9th or 10th century. The name 'Moray' can be traced back to the 10th or 11th century, when it related to a much larger region ruled by a Gaelic-speaking dynasty, the best-known member of which was Macbeth, king of Scots from 1040 to 1057.

Elgin is the county town of Moray and location of many places of interest that reflect its long history. King David I (r. 1124-1153) granted Elgin Royal Burgh status; in 1224 it became the seat of the Bishop of Moray. The Cathedral, although a ruin, is one of the finest examples of medieval architecture in Scotland. Castle remnants can still be seen on Lady Hill and the town centre boasts a fine array of houses that reflect the styles of successive eras. A new town trail, 'Castle to Cathedral to Cashmere' provides a

6   Sueno's Stone, floodlit.

guided tour through these sites of special interest.

The varied canvas of Moray is completed by its coastal strip that offers a wide variety of towns and villages. Most of these have their origins in the fishing industry, which is still active in some of them. Lossiemouth's magnificent beaches are a match for any seaside rival and so extensive that they are never crowded. The Moray Firth micro-climate extends its benevolent influence to this part of the coast and the waters of the firth are home to dolphins, seals and many species of seabirds. A very important part of the landscape and the economy is RAF Lossiemouth, the primary role of which is to provide aircraft for the 'Quick Reaction Alert (Interceptor) North' force. QRA is the Royal Air Force's front line defence of the UK 365 days a year.

So for residents and visitors alike, Moray provides something for everyone. The aim of this book is to give a taste of that variety and so encourage exploration, from mountain tops to seaside rocks – happy venturing!

Casks of aged whisky on display at The Glenlivet Distillery. 7

8   Founded in 1824 by George Smith, The Glenlivet Distillery is the home of one of the world's most famous malt whisky brands and is open to visitors for tours and tastings. It is one of eight distilleries

hat form the Malt Whisky Trail, the other members of which will be indicated by (MWT) where they appear in this book.

10 The village of Tomintoul, on the edge of the Glenlivet Crown Estate and in the Cairngorms foothills, is the highest village in the Highlands at around 355m/1160ft.

Moray has a share in Scotland's skiing industry at the *Lecht 2090*, as the road from Tomintoul passes 11
this ski and snowboard centre, located up in the hills on the border with Aberdeenshire.

12 The stream that flows out of Loch Avon continues its journey down Strath Avon, seen here near the scattered settlement of Fodderletter, north-west of Tomintoul.

Sited on a ridge above the confluence of the Rivers Livet and Avon, Drumin Castle occupies a **13** naturally strategic site. It is thought that Sir Walter Stewart built the current castle in the late 1400s.

14 Coming down Glenlivet, near the village of Tomnavoulin, it looks as though 'Daisy' is about to get a soaking from the approaching storm.

Further down Glenlivet by the B9008 is the Old Bridge of Livet. As built, it spanned the river **15** in three arches, one of which was washed away in the floods of 1829.

16 Attractively laid out Grantown-on-Spey, built to the plan of Sir James Grant, used to be in Moray and is the westernmost point in this book. The towered building is the former 19th-century orphanage.

Seen from the Grant Arms Hotel, this is the opposite view across The Square in Grantown. **17**
The town was laid out from 1765 and today is an ideal base for exploring the northern Cairngorms.

18 Winter can of course create some difficulties, but the compensation is the magical sight of snowy landscapes as seen here, a little to the south of Ballindalloch.

Tormore Distillery is not open to visitors but its attractive layout, complete with estate housing and an abundance of topiary, can be enjoyed from the road (A95) which passes close by.

20 Growth in the whisky industry is leading to new ventures such as Ballindalloch Distillery, which re-establishes the craft of distilling on the Ballindalloch Estate. It is open for tours for most of the year.

A little further along the river, Dalmunach is another new distillery, owned by Chivas Brothers. **21**
It is named after the nearby pool in the River Spey on whose banks the distillery sits.

22 Ballindalloch is one of the most beautiful and renowned castles in Scotland. Known as the Pearl of the North, it is located in the heart of Speyside, near to many famous whisky distilleries.

A much loved family home, Ballindalloch is one of the few privately owned castles to have been **23** lived in continuously by its original family. The Macpherson-Grants have resided there since 1546.

24 There is nothing like climbing the heights to appreciate the grandeur of the Speyside landscape. Taken from some of the granite outcrops on Ben Rinnes (see also pp. 30/31), this view looks

roughly north. The white building in the centre of the picture is Craigellachie Distillery, with Ben Aigan behind.

26 Continuing north up Speyside, Knockando Woolmill is a major new point of interest for visitors. The Category 'A' listed group of buildings date back to 1784. It has been lovingly restored over recent years

The Woolmill itself contains original textile machinery acquired over the centuries which remains **27** fully operational today and its products can be bought in the mill shop.

28 The Speyside Way long-distance walk stretches 65 miles from Aviemore to Buckie on the Moray coast (see pp.103/4). It uses sections of the former Speyside railway, as here at Tamdhu station.

Left: Cardhu Distillery (MWT) at Knockando was established officially in 1824. It is the only malt distillery pioneered by a woman. Right: near Marypark, this is Glenfarclas Distillery's Visitor Centre.

30 Outside of the Cairngorms, Ben Rinnes is the highest hill in Moray at 840m/2755ft. Pictured in the depths of winter, the summit is away to the left …

... from which magnificent views can be enjoyed, in this instance by the author's daughter. **31**
Ben Rinnes is not a demanding climb, taking about an hour-and-a-half at a modest pace.

32 Across the Spey from Ben Rinnes, over on the northern side of the strath, we come to the pleasing village of Archiestown, which was established 250 years ago.

Winters on Speyside are frequently harsh, as this February view of Archiestown shows. **33**
Ben Rinnes is in the distance.

34 The Spey between Aberlour and Craigellachie, a view which sums up Speyside: the river wrapped in the wooded hills with arable and livestock farming on its banks.

An autumn scene looking north-east across the village of Charlestown of Aberlour **35** with Ben Aigan (471m/1540ft) in the distance.

36 Aberlour Church of Scotland kirk. The settlement was developed in 1812 by Charles Grant of Wester Elchies, the Bi centenary of which is commemorated in the monument unveiled in 2012 (inset).

The Spey is one of Scotland's greatest salmon-fishing rivers, but it contains other fish too. **37**
This scene is near a fishing bothy between Craigellachie and Rothes.

38 The next village down river from Aberlour is Craigellachie, from where this precariously taken view from above Telford's bridge shows Speyside at its summer best.

The 200th anniversary of Craigellachie Bridge was celebrated in fine style in 2014, culminating in **39** this fireworks display above the bridge.

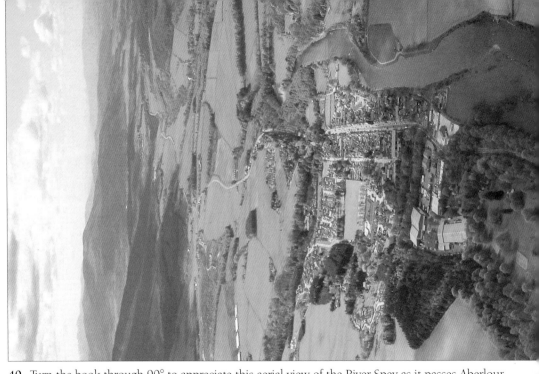

40 Turn the book through 90° to appreciate this aerial view of the River Spey as it passes Aberlour. It shows the neat plan to which the village was built. The group of large buildings is the HQ of

Walkers, the famous shortbread manufacturer. The picture on p.34 is looking along this stretch of the river from top to bottom.

42 Mountains of whisky casks at the Speyside Cooperage (just outside Craigellachie on the Dufftown road). Along with the eight distilleries, it is the ninth venue on the Malt Whisky Trail.

Going south-east from Craigellachie to Dufftown, this is Glenfiddich Distillery (MWT). It is little changed **43** since 1886, when William Grant and his nine children built the Distillery with their bare hands!

44 Balvenie Castle, Dufftown, was originally the seat of the powerful Comyn earls of Buchan. It is an enclosure castle with a massive curtain wall, now in the care of Historic Scotland.

Dufftown was founded in 1817 by James Duff, 4th Earl of Fife, and is a typical planned town **45** of the area with the main streets being laid out in the shape of a cross.

46 Mortlach Church, on the southern edge of Dufftown, is known for being one of the oldest sites of continuous Christian worship in Scotland, established by Molvag around 566.

Left: Auchindoun Castle stands in splendid isolation in the hills south of Dufftown. It is thought to ave been built by Thomas Cochrane, architect of James III, around 1480. Right: a view from the castle.

48 Returning northwards from Auchindoun to Speyside: the village of Rothes, home of three distilleries including Glen Grant, is seen here from the slopes of Ben Aigan across the valley.

Left: Glen Grant Distillery (MWT) is noted for its fine gardens complete with waterfall as well as its **49** excellent whisky. Right: a retired still at Glen Grant, with the Visitor Centre beyond.

50 Fochabers is a charming Speyside village north of Rothes, founded in 1776. Its recently restored ornamental fountain looks impressive against a backdrop of brilliant autumn colour.

Floral displays are another Fochabers speciality. This one is in recognition of Speyfest, **51** the village's annual music festival.

52 Fochabers is also home to Baxters Foods, where visitors have much to see including the Museum Shop (in background) and gardens with eye-catching features such as this stag sculpture.

The new star in the Fochabers firmament is Gordon Castle's Walled Garden. At eight acres it is the **53** largest producing walled garden in the country. Garden and Cafe (upper right) are pictured.

54 And finally, a few miles north of Fochabers, the River Spey flows into the sea between Spey Bay and Kingston (in the distance), 98 miles from its beginnings in the Monadhliath Mountains.

The Spey flows into the outer Moray Firth, well known for its Bottlenose dolphins. The organisation **55** Whale & Dolphin Conservation has a visitor centre at Spey Bay.

56 From its position on the Cluny Hills above Grant Park in Forres, the top of Nelson's Tower gives fine views in all directions, like this one of Findhorn Bay and village to the north of Forres.

58 Brodie Castle is near Moray's western border, close to Forres. This fine 16th-century tower house is packed with art and antiques. It is also famous for its many varieties of daffodils.

Logie Steading, in its tranquil, park-like setting, provides visitors with a place for both relaxation and exercise – browse the shops, walk along the Findhorn to Randolph's Leap or enjoy the gardens.

60 Logie House stands above Logie House Gardens. The house originates from the seventeenth century, since when it has evolved and grown. Similarly the garden has changed over the centuries.

Livestock at Logie: left upper: Longhorn cattle, the breed that originally made British beef famous, **61** are one of the oldest traditional breeds. Left lower: Jacob's sheep. Right: the beautiful River Findhorn.

62 Forres has been a Royal Burgh Town since about 1140. Left: the 70ft Nelson's Tower was erected in 1806 in celebration of Lord Nelson's victories. Right: Tolbooth Street in early morning quiet.

Left: the upper section of Forres Tolbooth, completed in 1849. Right: the Market Cross, **63** built in 1844, incorporates the base of an earlier, 17th century, cross.

64 *Forres in Bloom* has been creating floral masterpieces like this one in Grant Park for many years and has won five *Beautiful Scotland in Bloom* Awards and three from RHS *Britain in Bloom*.

Left: the Sunken Garden in Grant Park. Right: St Laurence's Church, built 1904-1906. Of the many ine buildings in Forres, this is perhaps the most impressive. The interior is worthy of inspection too.

66 Forres Highland Games are held annually. Among the many events are Tossing the Caber (left) and Hammer Throwing (right). Pipe bands also march and play – see p.112.

Benromach Distillery (MWT) is located on the northern edge of Forres. Although the smallest **67** working distillery in the Speyside area, it produces 150,000 – 250,000 litres of spirit per year.

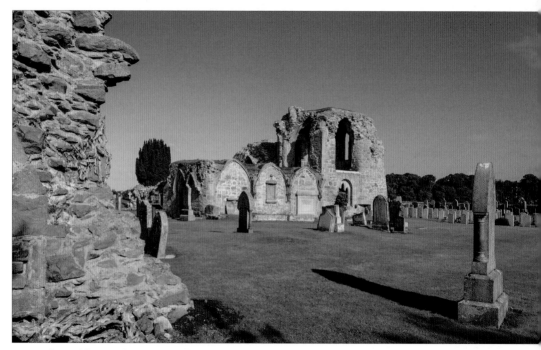

68 Kinloss Abbey is about two miles north-east of Forres. Founded in 1150 by the Cistercian Order, it became one of the most influential monasteries in Scotland until its demise in 1560.

Representing the modern face of Kinloss, the recently established Morayvia Interactive Sci-Tech Visitor **69** Centre has a fine range of aircraft exhibits, such as a Sea King helicopter and the nose of a Nimrod.

70 The former fishing village of Findhorn, four miles from Forres, has grown up around a large and sheltered bay. This view is near the village centre.

Compared with the picture on pp.56-57, this view gives a very different impression of **71**
Findhorn lagoon, a popular location for sailing boats of many kinds.

72 A few miles inland from Findhorn, Califer viewpoint provides grand panoramas to the west and north. This view looks roughly west across the coastal plain, the Moray Firth and the Black Isle

to snow-clad Ben Wyvis (1046m/3432ft), nearly 40 miles away in Easter Ross.

74 Going east from Findhorn we come to Burghead. This headland was once 'The biggest Iron Age fort in Britain', a Pictish stronghold from the 4th to 7th centuries. Pictured: remaining earthworks.

Burghead harbour still sees a certain amount of fishing activity. The nearby Visitor Centre **75** has displays that illustrate and interpret the Pictish Fort.

76 Another short step eastwards and we come to the pretty seaside village of Hopeman. It is noted for its flair for decoration such as these colourful beach huts. Inset: a ship weathervane.

Over on Hopeman's lovely west beach (the beach huts are at the east beach), it may be late March but distant Ben Wyvis still wears a good covering of snow.

78 A short distance inland from Hopeman stands Duffus Castle, the original seat of the De Moravia (Moray) family. One of the finest examples of a 12th-century motte and bailey castle in Scotland.

Located in the village of Duffus, Gordonstoun was founded in 1933 by Dr Kurt Hahn. Today's **79** School has all the facilities necessary to give it a lead in independent education in the 21st century.

80 Lossiemouth is Moray's main seaside town, established at the mouth of the River Lossie in the 18th century as a seaport for Elgin. This view is from the dunes on the east beach looking towards the town

Lossiemouth is a 'target-rich environment' for photographers. Above: two very different moods on **81** the west beach just after sunrise. Below: a mini-panorama shows off summer colours.

82 In mid-summer when the days are at their longest, the sun rises sufficiently far in the north-east so as to shine into this cave at the end of the west beach in Lossiemouth.

About half-an-hour later, this is the opposite view from the beach back towards the cavern, **83** with Covesea Lighthouse almost on top of the cave.

84 As noted in the introduction, RAF Lossiemouth is in the front line of Britain's air defences. To that end it is home to three squadrons of Typhoon jets. Poseidon maritime patrol aircraft will arrive in 2020.

Pluscarden Abbey is a few miles west of Elgin. Founded in 1230, it is the only medieval monastery **85** in Britain still inhabited by monks and being used for its original purpose. Visitors are welcome.

86 Glen Moray (MWT) has been distilling single malt whisky since 1897. On the western outskirts of Elgin, it is open to visitors for tours and tastings.

Elgin Castle, on Lady Hill, was a stronghold at a very early date and became a royal fortress in the 12th century. Some remains can still be seen at the top of the hill.

88 On the left is the remnant of the town house founded by the Bishops of Moray. The 15th-century
stone, defensible L-plan building possesses some pleasing architectural features. It was probably

the manse of the Cathedral Precentor. On the right stands the west end of the Cathedral itself. **89**
Established in 1224, it was laid waste by Alexander Stewart, the so-called Wolf of Badenoch, in 1390.

90 Left: the monument on Lady Hill was erected in 1839 to the memory of the fifth Duke of Gordon.
Right: the Muckle Cross and an ancient tower at the east end of the Plainstones in the centre of Elgin

The central square – or rather, oval – in Elgin is known as the Plainstones. Looking east, we see the 91 fountain, War Memorial and St Giles' Church flanked by mostly Victorian architecture.

92 Elgin's Cooper Park was gifted to the town by George Cooper in 1903. It is located to the north of the town centre and extends to the cathedral, just visible in the distance.

Appropriately sited next to the cathedral, the Biblical Garden is one of Elgin's more unusual attractions. Biblical scenes are recreated and all 110 plants mentioned in the Bible are featured.

94 Snowy winter nights can produce a unique mood. Here we see the Bishop's House looking very different from its appearance on p.88.

The remains of Elgin Cathedral, viewed from the east and looking towards the west-end towers.
Its many outstanding features include the country's finest octagonal chapter house.

96 Independently run since 1797, Johnston's has been making beautiful knitwear, clothing and accessories from the most luxurious wools known to man for over two centuries.

Just north of Elgin is Spynie Palace, residence of the Bishops of Moray for five centuries. Its location **97** was chosen because, when built in the 1200s, it was on the coast, now two miles to the north.

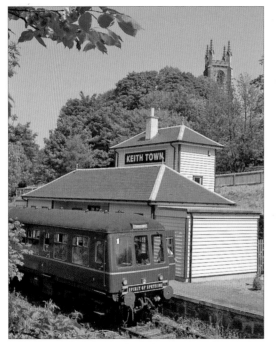

98 The market town of Keith straddles the Isla river. Left: a Keith & Dufftown preserved railway train at Keith Town station. Right: Keith War Memorial.

Strathisla Distillery (MWT) goes way back to 1786, although it was not until the 1870s that this name was applied. Its annual capacity is 2.4 million litres of spirit.

100 The Auld Brig over the River Isla in Keith was built in 1609 by Thomas Murray and his wife Janet Lindsay, reputedly in memory of their son who drowned while trying to cross the river.

This delightful and clever monument to the war-time efforts of the Landgirls is at Clochan, **101** between Fochabers and Buckie. Designed by Peter Naylor, it looks equally 'right' from either side!

102 An atmospheric seascape taken on a windy evening from Port Gordon, which lies a little to the east of Buckie.

Buckie was the largest town in the old county of Banff and is one of the largest in Moray. Left: the **103** Episcopal Church, Cluny Square. Right: War Memorial. The Speyside Way starts/ends in Buckie.

104 The fine old sailing ship *Regina Caelis* is berthed in Buckie's Cluny Harbour which was completed in 1880.

A few miles east of Buckie is Findochty, a particularly attractive coastal village. It is an ancient **105** settlement, referred to as far back as the mid 10th century.

106 Findochty (pronounced Fin-ech-tay) harbour, in some ways like others in the county, and yet offering a scene that is unique.

This aerial view of Portknockie, the next village east, shows that it is a well-planned village, **107** laid out as neatly as the landscape allows.

108 The Bow Fiddle Rock is Portknockie's most visited attraction. It looks especially dramatic when seen against a backdrop of the Aurora Borealis.

The pleasing town of Cullen is last stop on this journey through Moray. Here, the sunny day is **109** threatened by an explosion of cumulus clouds bubbling up over the town.

110 The view through the old railway arch up Seafield Street towards the town centre.

These rocky remnants known as the Three Kings continue to defy the elements on Cullen beach. **111**
The coastline continues of course, but that takes us into the territory of another journey . . .

Published 2019 by Lyrical Scotland, an imprint of Lomond Books Ltd, Broxburn, EH52 5NF
www.lyricalscotland.com www.lomondbooks.com

Originated by Ness Publishing, 47 Academy Street, Elgin, Moray, IV30 1LR
First published by Ness Publishing 2009. 2nd edition 2011, reprinted 2013. 3rd edition 2016.

Printed in China

All photographs © Colin and Eithne Nutt except p.21 © Chivas Brothers; p.23 © Ballindalloch Castle;
p.27 © Knockando Woolmill; p.29 (left) © Diageo; pp.40/41 & 107 © Scotavia Images; p.55 © Charlie Phillips;
p.69 © Jim Simpson; p.79 © Gordonstoun School; p.98 (left) © Keith & Dufftown Railway;
p.108 © Francis Masson, snuBBachub photography; back cover © Mark Power, MAGNUM PHOTOS

Text © Colin Nutt
ISBN 978-1-78818-075-7

Front cover: Elgin Cathedral; p.1: leaping salmon sculpture in Fochabers; p.4: the Landgirls monument near Buckie;
this page: massed bands at Forres Highland Games; back cover: the new Macallan Distillery